Writing Doesn't Have to Be Lonely

14 Ways to Get
the Help of Other
People When
You Write

Lawrence Weinstein

OneOfaKind Books
1770 Massachusetts Ave., Suite 215
Cambridge, MA 02140

Bookstore Managers and Buyers
To order copies, please either
call 617-866-0875
or go to our special website for placing orders:
www.OneOfaKindBooks.com.

Photo credit, cover and page 52 – Carlos Almendarez

ISBN 978-0-615-65160-6

Table of Contents

Introduction

You would have no need for this book if you were more like a leopard. That stealthy cat spends most of life alone and likes it that way. Because he counts on silence for catching his prey, he doesn't want other members of his species socializing with him.

By contrast, we human beings are born to interact with each other. We live in families. We go to work at places that have a thousand names on the payroll. We join congregations, clubs, and overlapping friendship groups. We arrange even to be buried close to other creatures of our own kind.

One big reason many people dread to write (dread it worse than being buried, I think) is that their writing habits don't satisfy their inborn need for company. In the forty years since I began teaching writing at the college level, the number of students I have met who genuinely like to be secluded with their writing—who are as happy as a leopard to hole themselves up somewhere for the duration—comes, perhaps, to ten. This is a book for everyone else.

In a nutshell, your writing will go best when you alternate the solitary times with times of companionship and sharing.

Not only will you enjoy yourself more, but your finished products will come out better.

The sharing, "social" times might occur before you put a single word down, or they might occur when you've got a whole draft in hand. As you will discover in the pages that follow, all phases that you go through to produce a paper—every step from brainstorming for a topic to proofreading—can benefit from the involvement of another person.

This is not a book just about the company and help available for writing at school, either. Although most of the examples in it pertain to your role as a student, the array of types of help described here should prove valuable to you long after graduation. It applies to producing effective...

- application letters for jobs
- memos and reports once you land a job
- blog posts
- poems, lyrics, and short stories
- toasts at family occasions
- public talks
- ads
- and countless other forms of writing that your life will

demand of you or inspire you to do.

You can both increase the fun of writing and improve as a writer in all realms of life by making it a habit to invite peers into your writing process.

Lawrence Weinstein

A Note About the Word "Helper"

Because the individuals available to you for company and help in writing will go by different names—"tutor," "friend," "classmate" during the school years, and "coworker," "editorial consultant," etc. later on—I have called your helper by different names in this book. Often, I have just said "helper," so as to keep things simple.

#1

Making a Writing "Date"

One simple way to eliminate the loneliness of writing is to do it near one or more people who are simultaneously doing it, too. Set a time with a tutor, classmate, or friend to literally be in the same room while you and that person forge ahead on your respective writing projects. (One of you might have a research paper to work on; the other, a flyer for a campus activity—that part doesn't matter.) Think of the occasion as a writing "date."

I have never worked as a reporter on a big daily newspaper, but some movies I've seen suggest that human sociability is one of the unspoken attractions of the job—the experience of doing one's writing in the midst of fellow writers. Such experience goes a long way toward explaining my enjoyment of the several writing workshops I've attended in my time. Just hearing others around me making their keyboards click—or their pens skirr—relieves me of anxiety. It's a flow that I'm enticed to join in.

1. Before actually setting your writing date, ask the person who might be joining you what her optimal working conditions are, to be sure that you and she are compatible writers. Does she need silence while you need heavy metal? That may mean you need to bring your iPod. Does she tend to write for two or three hours at a stretch, while you need breaks every twenty minutes? That could be a deal-breaker, depending on how unobtrusively you take your breaks. If necessary, find another writing partner, somebody whose writing habits are in better synch with yours.

2. At least occasionally, take breaks at the same time as your partner, to apprise her of how it's going. Having someone to check in with—someone to vent to when the words don't come, and to celebrate with when they start flowing—is part of the appeal.

   On the other hand, keep your comments brief, in order not to rob yourself or your partner of momentum

3. Is it a good idea to make a writing date with somebody who attracts you romantically? I don't

know, having never made a writing date like that myself. I imagine it might go either way: it might increase your comfort level or, in fact, destroy it. It could lead to a relaxed, productive state of concentration or to nonstop distraction. If you'd like to go that route, just be forewarned.

A Note to Helpers

- The writing "date" is the first of many opportunities described in this book for you to benefit as much as the writer you work with. If a classmate or friend proposes that the two of you have this kind of session together, think of the papers *you* need to write soon — or of the screenplay, letter to the editor of your campus weekly, etc. that *you* would like to write —and prepare to use the date as *your* excuse to get started.

- If you are a writing center tutor, you may well not know when such a "date" is coming up, since people use your center for a wide variety of purposes and often just drop in. If you're a tutor, always try to have on hand a draft-in-progress of your own to pull out for unannounced "dates."

#2

Getting Mentored

Have you been told, "Never use contractions in a paper"? Here is what an upperclassman has to say about that dictum:

> This is a rule high school teachers pounded into your head because they wanted you to formalize your writing style. That's all well and good, but you must know when formal tone is appropriate and when it's not. Legal documents and wedding invitations should not contain contractions. If you're writing a regular essay, try to limit them to make your writing sound more mature. But if you have a loose and easy personality, don't make your writing sound fake and awkward by using "cannot" every time in place of "can't." You can use contractions, just in moderation.*

One wise use of a writing helper—if that person is a student who has more experience at your school than you have—is to get him or her to "show you the ropes," to give you some guidance and spare you some beginner's mistakes. A veteran helper can play the role of mentor. The block quote above is an example of what mentoring sounds like.

Students arrive at college with their minds reverberating with a wide variety of **rules about writing**. Some of these rules—like "Never use contractions"—are too simple. Some don't apply at all in the years after high school. Some are spot on. That's where mentoring comes in.

Here's a short quiz for you. Below, I have listed just four of the numerous rules that many first-year students still accept and live by. Would you be able to confidently label each one either "too simple," "wrong," or "right"?

> A teacher who assigns you a paper to write generally wants you to use it to show an understanding of the teacher's own point of view, and to agree with it.

> The best way to organize a paper is to follow the sequence of the Five-Paragraph Theme.

> Never say "I" in academic writing.

> In a paper, the bigger the word the better—as long as it has the right meaning.

In conversation with a mentor, you could *check out the validity* of rules like these. Find out which, if any, hold true at the college you're enrolled at. (Can you tell which rule a writer and her helper are discussing in the series of photos on page 14?)

Also with a mentor's help, you could master crucial **terminology**. Maybe, for example, certain words used in a government course assignment confuse you, such as "case study" or "analyze." A good mentor could define or illustrate them for you.

In addition, if you're not familiar with the **graceful turns** a proficient student writer makes — for example, to move from a summary of views expressed in an assigned reading to a statement of the student's own views — a good mentor could teach you those turns. (Did you know, for instance, of the widely employed Set-up-and-Reject form of paper-writing, in which the writer starts out by acknowledging at length an author's beliefs and reasoning — respectfully, to show that there's intelligence at work there — but eventually proceeds to point out problems with the author's argument and to replace it with something better? A mentor might provide you with both (a) a stock of phrases to use to set such a paper in motion — like "To hear Ann Smith tell of it, the U.S. economy is doomed" — and (b) a stock of phrases to use to navigate the turn to your own position — like "On closer inspection, however, Smith's argument proves deeply flawed." Learning just that one, potent maneuver would make the task of finding a mentor worthwhile.)

And a good mentor could explain your school's policies on **plagiarism**—for example, the difference between "common knowledge" (like the year Columbus discovered America, which doesn't call for any reference to a source) and factual material requiring citation.

Other questions for a mentor will have less to do with *standard* practice and more to do with **personal preferences of your instructors**: "Does Rodriguez let you say 'I' in papers? Does she object to contractions?" When you get that specific, even a good mentor won't always have the answers you seek, and you'll sometimes need to put the questions to your instructors themselves. On some occasions, though, your mentor will know.

Finally, if you are lucky, your mentor will be able to comment not just on the proper form of written "products" (that is, papers and the like), but on the ***process* of writing**. He might urge you, for example, to put your first draft of a paper away in a drawer for a day or more, to improve your ability to bring fresh eyes to it when you revise it.

1. Play the field awhile. Try out a few tutors at your writing center—or a classmate who appears to be as generous as he is smart, or (if you live on campus) an upperclassman in your dorm or fraternity—until you find yourself a mentor whose chemistry with you is good and who provides you guidance of the kind described above.

2. *If you get advice that doesn't square with personal experience, don't follow it.* I once encountered a student who'd begin work on a paper not by settling on what to say in it, but by deciding how many paragraphs it should contain and how many sentences each paragraph should have—in the same way that a poet might decide to write a sonnet (a poem of fourteen lines following a regular rhyme scheme) or a haiku (a Japanese poetic form of three lines and fixed syllable counts). I had never heard of such a practice on the part of a prose writer, but it worked for her—just as rigid verse forms work for many poets—and, in fact, her coming to the writing

center had nothing to do with that step in her process of writing. Who was I to challenge it or call it into question? A writer should be free to do what works. Don't let anyone deprive you of that right.

* from a handout by writing center tutor Rob Mills

A Note to Helpers

"Mentor" doesn't mean the same thing as "expert." Don't refrain from mentoring another, less experienced writer just because you don't have expertise on all writing matters. When you need to, reach unapologetically for a handbook, or even text a friend who knows more about the aspect of writing in question. The person you are mentoring is sure to appreciate your honesty about your own limits, as well as your willingness to be of assistance in *getting* him the answers he needs.

> A Place to Keep Your Own List of Questions for a Mentor

....

....

....

....

....

....

....

....

....

....

....

....

....

#3

Pacing Yourself—with Help

In discussing writing tips that a good mentor would give you (page 18 above), I offered the example of putting your first draft away for a while, so that you can return to it with fresh eyes before revising it. That's a writing habit that has always yielded quite surprising, positive results, but it depends on something I have yet to mention: time. If a writer doesn't finish the first draft of a paper until the night before the paper itself is due, obviously there's no time to give that draft a rest before revising it...and possibly no time for revising at all.

Unfortunately, many papers get written the night before they're due, when no opportunity is left to do work of high quality.

Another way to use a second person is as someone to check in with at predetermined points in the writing process, to ensure that you are *spreading out* the process. It's like setting multiple due dates for yourself—a date by which to have decided on a writing topic, a date by which to have assembled research materials (if it's a research paper that you're working on), a date by which to have come up with a trial thesis...and so forth. Knowing there is someone who actually expects you to touch base with him or her at all those junctures—even for two minutes—can be highly motivating; it has more force than promises made only in your own head.

At times, I myself still use a check-in schedule that way, if I am in danger of procrastinating. Recently, for a long report I had to write about the working conditions of adjunct faculty, I deliberately announced to all the adjuncts whom I'd inter-viewed that I would have a draft to them for their review by a certain date well in advance of the time I was expected to formally submit my report. That promise worked. It got me off to an early start.

A famous French chef was reportedly once asked for his secret ingredient. He replied, "Time." That's how I feel about writing.

Try This ›

When is your next paper due?

Here's a list of possible steps in a good writing process. Check as many as you'd like to make part

of your work on the upcoming paper—but include
at least two more steps than you take normally:

- [ ] brainstorming for a question or topic to address in
  your paper

- [ ] free-writing your first thoughts on the question or
  topic, based on things you already know about it,
  or relevant experience you've already had

- [ ] assembling your research materials

- [ ] making arrangements for types of research other
  than reading, such as interviewing or conducting
  an experiment

- [ ] starting a project journal or a stack of index cards
  for putting down facts, observations, and reflec-
  tions on your question or topic

- [ ] developing a trial thesis

- [ ] trying out that trial thesis on a classmate, friend,
  or writing center tutor

- [ ] creating an outline for your paper

- [ ] trying out that outline on a classmate, friend,
  or tutor

- [ ] producing a first draft of your paper

- [ ] giving that draft a rest for two days

☐ revising

☐ trying out your revised draft on a classmate, friend, or tutor

☐ revising one more time—and proofreading

☐ turning in your paper.

How many steps have you checked? Five or six? Ten?

How much time is left until your final due date? With that length of time in mind, decide how many days you can afford to give each of your steps. *For each step you've checked, enter the date by which you aim to have completed that step.*

Finally, decide exactly whom to ask to be your "pacer." Give that person a copy of your schedule.

Now just hold to it, if you can! Does your enjoyment of the writing process go up? What about the value of the final product?

A Personal Note on the First Step Above: Brainstorming for a Topic

All too often, students whose instructors give them latitude in determining a paper topic settle for the first topic that occurs to them, regardless of how little they might care about it. I was once visited at the Bentley University Writing Center by a student whose expository writing teacher had assigned her to write a short essay on "one thing all your jobs for pay and volunteer positions have had in common." The student seized on the first common denominator that occurred to her: all of her jobs had been indoors. That might have made a fine topic for this student if, for example, she had been an outdoors person who always felt cooped up at work—or an indoors person who felt grateful not to have to labor in the noonday sun like her siblings on the family farm—but she was neither of these things; she hardly cared at all about the indoor-outdoor distinction, and her paper showed it. After she accepted my suggestion that we go back to scratch with her paper and begin by spending longer to discover a topic that mattered to her, my role was mainly to give her support, keeping her going with lines like "Good idea. Do you have others? Think about what else might be involved in doing the jobs you've had"—until she managed to come up with a topic that meant a lot to her: in all her jobs, she had had to hold her temper. It had taken forty-five minutes or an hour, but now she had a topic that unquestionably hit a nerve. One telling anecdote after another came pouring out. She literally went from writing a paper that bored her and me to writing one of the most absorbing student papers I have read, and the key was making ample time in her process to brainstorm extensively.

If, like her, you need company for brainstorming, you could use a writing helper in the same way she used me.

#4

Having a Sounding Board

So far in this book, you've encountered three big reasons people need each other—not just when they write, but generally in life:

- we crave company (as in Chapter 1: Making a Writing "Date")

- we depend on having knowledge handed down to us (as in Chapter 2: Getting Mentored)

- we sometimes need to be held accountable to our own plans (as in Chapter 3: Pacing Yourself).

For a few pages that start now (covering Chapters 4-6), you'll encounter a big reason for needing each other that will probably surprise you:

- we have to play.

I don't mean physical play. I am not referring to throwing balls. I mean play of mind—I mean bouncing ideas off another person. We are such thoroughly social creatures, it often requires "going back and forth with someone else" to activate our own intelligence.

The kind of human interplay I mean comes in two forms: sounding board style and devil's advocate style. These are not at all the same. Someone acting as your sounding board supports the progress of your thinking in a nurturing fashion; a devil's advocate tries to poke holes in your thinking. Which one you need depends on your temperament and where in the writing process you find yourself at the moment.

I'll save your devil's advocate for the next chapter.

A human sounding board either listens to you talk your ideas out or gets them from an outline or a set of notes you provide. She attempts to understand your thinking and to paraphrase it. "I see what you're saying," says your sounding board. "The number of planets like Earth in the universe is so huge that even if the odds of life existing on an Earth-like planet are one in a million, that would still mean there's probably life on some of them." A sounding board acknowledges and validates the work of your mind by taking pains to follow it. By itself, that kind of attentiveness is often enough to sustain a writer through the whole pre-writing phase of developing a paper.

Does a sounding board always confine herself to restating your ideas or acknowledging them? No, but when she gets around to giving you reactions to them—or plies you with questions about them—she remains respectful of both you and your mind. She knows that in addition to feedback, you need support. (She also knows that you've expended more time and thought on the topic of your paper than she has.) Therefore, she imparts her feedback tentatively. In all matters where the two of you think differently, she defers to you without a fight. She might say, "The only part of your idea about life in the universe that I don't follow is your computation. Maybe that's *my* problem." Or she might say, "I notice that you don't *define* 'life' in your draft. When you say 'life in the universe,' what do you mean—life as we know it, or something broader?"

If you go so far as to ask your sounding board whether you've convinced her of your point, she might answer in the negative. Even then, however, she would choose her words with care, in order to continue to support you as your thinking develops. She might say, "Not yet."

Try This ›

1. On your next paper, get an early enough start to find and use a sounding board for your ideas.

2. Whether you approach a classmate, friend, or tutor, *be explicit* about what you're seeking. If

you don't want the services of a devil's advocate, you'll need to say so. You'll need to say, "What I need is honest reactions—but not from someone who is unsupportive or who feels he knows my subject better than I do. I need someone who can draw me out, who can keep me going as I try to think more fully on the question I'm dealing with."

A Note to Helpers

Being Someone's Sounding Board

For me at least, the most consequential point in someone's writing process comes right after he has done all his reading or research. It's the point at which he starts to formulate what it all adds up to.

Don't rush a writer through this crucial phase. On the contrary, make it last. Make it yield the kind of first-rate thinking that will stand the writer in good stead when the time arrives for drafting.

Some advice for you:

1. Most writers—students included—have the ability to think a lot more extensively about their topics than they normally do.

For some of these "under-performing thinkers," all that's required from a helper like yourself is a pair of good ears inclined in their direction. The psychologist Bill Perry used to tell of a teacher of his who, in their periodic conferences, drew more and more out of him just by avidly going "Huh!" "Well!" and "You don't say!" as young Bill put forth his half-formed ideas. The effect on motivation should hardly surprise us. Is there any feedback more reinforcing than another person's active and respectful interest?

An alternative way to show interest and keep the writer going is the approach illustrated on page 30, in the example about life on other planets: **paraphrase combined with requests for clarification.**

2. **With other writers, more is called for.** Some don't understand that, generally speaking, writing a paper requires something quite different from regurgitating so-called "right answers," the positions taken by an instructor or the author of an assigned text. What it requires is inquiry, a process that involves three moves of the mind: **questioning, hypothesizing, and testing.** You can do a writer a great service by self-consciously

listening for all three moves in a sounding board session, and by prompting any move you don't hear the writer already making.

What do these moves sound like? I'll try to give you some idea.

questioning

In writing a paper, all that is likely to result without a question is a dump of loosely related facts and ideas. Only a question gives thought direction. In a recent conversation at my writing center, a student told me she already knew the question that she wanted to address in a paper: "Does thought require language?" With that, she was off and running.

If she had not arrived so well focused—if, for instance, she had said, "I need to write a paper that has something to do with thought and language"—I would have slowed way down. Recognizing that no question had been formulated yet, I'd have started prompting her for one by saying things like the following:

...Is there a mystery for you regarding thought and language?

...In your reading, what controversies or questions about thought and language piqued your interest?

...Did any of the claims made in your reading seem less-than-convincing to you? Which ones? Why? Can you translate one of your doubts about a claim into an interesting question?

hypothesizing

Not long after framing a question, the engaged writer starts framing possible answers to it, known as hypotheses. A hypothesis may well be wrong (usually it *is* wrong, or in need of refinement), but it's invaluable. By giving the writer an idea to test, it gives her traction. I asked the student who was wondering if thought requires language, "What's your first, gut response to the question?" and she replied by defining thought as "statement-making in the mind"—which, of course, implied that language is required.

Other ways I might have prompted a hypothesis from her include the line:

...If you had to make a stab at an answer right now, what would it be?

testing

When inquiry is genuine—when it's about more than cranking out a paper for a passing grade—the writer eagerly subjects her first hypothesis to a meaningful test: she puts it right alongside facts that might tend either to confirm it or to call it into question. She doesn't pre-select her facts; she understands that it's the "inconvenient" ones that will impel her thinking forward, toward a *better* answer. The student wondering if thought requires language was a genuine inquirer. She pulled hard for inconvenient facts, and she found plenty. To begin with, she recalled that even a newborn—who possesses no language—effectively solves problems facing it, such as how to maneuver to the right part of its mother's anatomy to maximize the intake of milk! Wisely, she went on to replace her first definition of thought with a definition that did not involve language: the ability to perceive patterns. Even that definition, she punctuated with a question mark—a sign that she wasn't done testing.

Some lines to prompt testing include:

...What facts available to you seem to support that answer?

...More importantly, can you think of facts that don't fit that answer neatly or at all?

*...You've had quite a lot to say on this question today. Does any of it make you think you need to **change** your initial thesis?*

*...How could you be more **certain** of your answer? For example, might it help to do more reading or research before we meet again?*

and, if the above gambits don't elicit much...

...How does your answer jibe with _____?
[Fill in the blank either with an "inconvenient" fact that occurs to you, the helper, or, in the case of a controversy, with a point made by the opposing side.]

Why Writers Won't Notice that You're Following This Sequence

If you learn to use it casually and deftly, the results of the q/h/t sequence (questioning, hypothesizing, testing) will be dramatic, and, hard as you may find it to believe, the writer will not have a clue that you've been following a protocol. Why? Because the q/h/t sequence (otherwise known as inquiry) is a mental activity she was literally born to perform. She engages in it in her home and on the street many times daily.

Here is an example adapted from my own experience. (For numerous other examples, see books by cognitive psychologists like John Dewey and David N. Perkins.)

questioning

A friend passes you on campus and you greet her warmly, but she doesn't return your greeting. You are left to wonder, "Why didn't Samantha say hello?"

hypothesizing

Quickly (in fact, virtually at lightning speed, you come so well equipped for these operations of the mind), you recall that people tend not to respond unless they know they are being addressed, and you say to yourself, "Maybe she didn't hear me."

testing

Did Samantha *look* as if she hadn't heard?

If your first answer fills the bill, inquiry ends.
Samantha may never have made eye contact with
you. She may have seemed distracted, as if she
had some pressing business to see to. In addition,
you may now recall her telling you yesterday that
she would be going to a job interview at about
this time today. That would settle that: she *hadn't*
heard.

*If, however, your initial answer fails to survive
this test—or survives, but along with other
plausible hypotheses, which haven't yet been
tested—you plunge on.* Admit it: Samantha's
neglect of your greeting may have been
deliberate; she seemed to face away from you
at just that tilt and angle life has taught you to
associate with disdain or hurt feelings. You must
think harder. Could Samantha have taken offense
at some action of yours? Is she aggrieved that you
disputed a point of hers in class yesterday?

*When you can't be sure of an answer based on
information you already have, you devise a way
to obtain more information.* Assuming you expect

to see Samantha later in the week, you decide to
note exactly how she greets you then.

What could be more natural than such a train of
thought?

---

3. **The one kind of sounding board session I would
   like to caution against is the type that in reality
   short-circuits thinking.** In this kind, the classmate,
   friend, or tutor not only fails to *prevent* a timid
   writer's "rush past thinking" but actually prompts
   it and facilitates it. The questions posed by
   helpers working in this way typically include:

   "What's your thesis?" ...but that question makes
   a writer feel he should already have come up with
   a good answer to his paper's question—that is, it
   cues the writer to start outlining his paper.

   "Do you have examples to back your thesis up?"
   ...but this question tacitly suggests that the only
   facts of use to a writer are the ones that appear
   to *support* his first answer to the question he's
   addressing, whereas usually the facts that advance
   inquiry are the troublesome ones, the ones that
   lead a writer to discover that his current answer

needs to be discarded or substantially modified.

"Have you come up with a good introduction?"
"How about a conclusion?"
...but like the two preceding questions, these don't pertain as much to the problem of generating thought as to the problem of reporting it engagingly once it's taken place.

The function of a sounding board is to promote thought-generation. Questions like these put the cart before the horse; they properly belong to a later stretch of the writing process. (See Chapter 8.)

5

Having a Devil's Advocate

Your sounding board (pages 29-32 above) *pulls* for more from you, on the assumption you already "have more in you." He is always telling you, implicitly, "*You have what it takes* to think more fully, more extensively." A devil's advocate, by contrast, is an intellectual bully. He doesn't pull, he pushes. He doesn't mollycoddle you: he confronts you, dares you. He's not someone you would want to meet in a dark alley...or on a blog.

If you have a sturdy ego (but that's a big "if"), you can benefit as much from a rude and ruthless devil's advocate as from a good sounding board. Both can be invaluable but at different points in time—the sounding board early in the writing process, while you're still getting your bearings, and the devil's advocate later in the process—maybe even after you've completed a first draft—when you are liable to be too impressed by the sound of your own words to realize they're masking a flawed argument. After trying out both types of responders, you should decide which of them to work into your own writing process, as well as *when* to work them in.

For your interest, there is a good reason why a true devil's advocate shows no mercy. Any praise—even faint praise, like "You make some good points here, Laura, but…"—compromises the intended spirit of the role. The only way to minimize the risk that you will be demoralized by your devil's advocate is to prohibit him from uttering anything *but* criticism. You need to be able to tell yourself, "*Of course* the devil's advocate had nothing nice to say about my thinking: playing nice is not allowed."

In response to your thoughts on a Robert Frost poem, a good devil's advocate might say,

> What?! You call Frost "America's greatest poet"?! Was he really better than Walt Whitman or than T.S. Eliot? I don't see your basis for that claim.
>
> or
>
> This interpretation of the poem is so simple-minded. It ignores the whole last stanza—probably because that stanza wouldn't fit into your thesis.
>
> or
>
> I disagree with you that Frost's rhymes "add to the poem's meaning." They just make the poem more fun to read…or easier to memorize. They're like ornaments.

Comments such as these may be right or wrong—they may not even reflect the devil's advocate's real views. Their function is to drive your thinking on. You must either do a better job of defending your position or change it to accommodate objections that the "devil" has convinced you are legitimate.

Try This ›

1. In recruiting your devil's advocate, go for the tutor, classmate, or friend who is generally sharp about things and has at least a basic familiarity with your subject. Once again, spell out expectations: Use the *term* "devil's advocate." *Stipulate* that praise of any kind is out of bounds, and that what you want is negativity.

2. Usually it's helpful for a devil's advocate to state his objections at length, but that's not always necessary. I had an agent once who went through my draft of a book writing the word "Nah" in the margin wherever he had trouble accepting what I was saying. "Nah" was enough. Knowing (by then) something of how his mind worked, I was able in each case to surmise what the problem with my logic was, and to deal with it either by admitting I was wrong or by supplying necessary links of thought I had left out. The result was a much stronger book.

Engaging in a Silent Dialogue

A Variant Approach to Either #4 or #5

I've met people who have no trouble talking but dread the act of writing. Are you like that? If so...

Try This >

1. When meeting with a writing helper to do preliminary thinking for a paper, adopt the rule of silence. In a silent dialogue, have your helper ply you with all the same questions that spur you to develop ideas fully in a sounding board session (Chapter 4 above) or a devil's advocate session (Chapter 5 above). The only difference is that you and he shouldn't speak at all; your thoughts should go directly from your head to the page or computer screen.

The advantages of silent dialogue are twofold: (1) It builds up *pressure* to write. Everybody wants to communicate. If a person's usual means of expression, the mouth, becomes unavailable, he or she will suddenly *want* to write. (2) In the course of writing what he usually speaks out loud, a person will find writing less and less alien as an activity. It will come more naturally.

In tangible terms, the result of silent dialogue is an intellectually lively transcript—and the words that comprise it remain available to you (since they're written down) as a kind of pre-first draft. Their unrehearsed vitality will be intact.

Here goes the beginning of a silent dialogue I had with an undergraduate who wanted to use writing to ponder the question "Is college worth it financially?"

Helper: What a question! Where is it coming from?

Writer: I suppose it has been building, but it was ignited by reading the book *Rich Dad, Poor Dad* last week.

Helper: What does the author say that set you down this track of thought?

Writer: The author learned from life. He joined the Navy and put himself through college later in life. By the age of 47 he retired as a millionaire, and by no fluke. He took every job and experience as a learning opportunity. With that in mind, I can't help but wonder if I would have been better off working (and learning while working) than at college.

Helper: So then that's the question, more precisely. (I've underlined it just to track it.) How are you tempted to answer it at the moment?

Writer: On the one hand, I know financially I'd be better off. Considering the wages that I'm losing by not working—and the high amount I'm losing in tuition costs, etc.—financially it seems ludicrous to be here. On the other hand, I have to wonder if I'd even be thinking these thoughts, had I not gone to college. Opportunities to learn and profit may have simply passed me by, had I not had three years here to become financially literate.

Helper: There seems to be a lot embedded in each of your conflicting feelings. But to start with the first: Can you spell out more specifically the facts you've gotten from experience or reading that suggest you pay a big opportunity cost to attend college? Is it primarily the one author's story?

Writer: For example, if I wanted to go into real estate, I might have spent two years in construction and a year in a real estate office. I could have begun to learn the industry instead of taking a class on strategic management. Not to mention that in those years I could have earned a salary of $30,000 to $40,000 per year, instead of being $75,000 in the hole from college loans....

> As you can probably tell, the dialogue was merely getting rolling at this point. By the end, the writer surfaced many counter-arguments and complications (and, by the way, decided not to leave school). He told me that the dialogue had been his first good chance to think the matter out.

2. Some parts of the dialogue above could have been cut and pasted, then expanded on, revised... until they made good sections of an actual paper. Look at your own silent dialogue for passages to use that way.

Also look for passages that fall short as writing but contain *ideas* that are worth keeping. During the drafting phase, find better language for expressing those ideas.

Finally, take note of gaps in your thinking that will need filling.

A Note to Helpers

- In a silent dialogue, it's imperative to keep the use of mouths to a minimum. If the writer lapses into speech—maybe laughing and saying, "This is so hard"—rather than *reply* in speech, reply on the page, maybe writing, "Yeah, we're not used to communicating this way with a person sitting right in front of us." By remaining in writing mode yourself, you improve the chances that your conversation partner will do likewise.

- Don't leave a writer alone at the table, even if her turn to write in silence is taking a long time. Your leaving could feel like abandonment to her—or like lack of interest in what she has to say. Stay where you are and browse in a book or newspaper until your next turn. Or, better yet, anticipate what your next contribution to the dialogue might be.

- Keep your own contributions to the dialogue relatively brief.

- Your contributions should be of the sounding board kind (pages [29-32] above), as in the sample dialogue about whether to stay at college—unless the writer has expressly asked you to play devil's advocate (pages [43-45] above).

#7

Hearing Your Words on Another's Lips

I have a certain colleague who has told me several times that he pities me for being a playwright. (Plays are not all that I write, but I do write plays.) He claims that as a poet and essayist he is in complete control of how his writing comes across, whereas playwrights like myself are at the mercy of directors and actors, who often misunderstand our words and render them aloud in ways that defeat our intentions.

I tell that colleague that he's fooling himself. Yes, I have been mortified at times to hear actors garble my lines— or, even worse, take a line that's serious and play it for laughs—but that doesn't mean that people aren't garbling his lines, too: it just means that as a playwright I get to *hear* the garbling, and he doesn't. Because people generally read essays and poems privately—and silently—he is being spared the telltale signs of their confusion.

When it comes down to it, I would rather hear than not

hear. I would rather know what havoc my words are producing in another person's head than remain ignorant of it. By knowing what's gone wrong in the transmission from me to someone else, I can tell what needs revising.

In fact, essay writers shouldn't pity playwrights, they should envy them, since playwrights have a natural feedback loop built into the process of refining their work. *All* writers need that.

One good way you can obtain such feedback on a paper is to arrange a "performance" of it—a time when a good reader will read your draft out loud in your hearing. If that good reader is reading for meaning, striving to make sense of what she reads, her voice will automatically register a lot of what you need to know:

- A pause between sentences that lasts abnormally long (especially a pause accompanied by a furrowed brow) might indicate that your logic isn't clear.

- Vocal emphasis thrown to a word you would not have stressed can be a sign that you have not distinguished your main point from minor ones.

- Running past an intended break in a line—for example, saying (in a rush) "Before that time" in a sentence that was meant to go, "Before that, time was not an issue"—almost always marks the place where a comma's missing.

1. To get yourself the right reader, be on the lookout for a person who has both intelligence and a free, expressive voice. Even then, be explicit that you want him or her to read for meaning, not just to recite words on the page.

2. Definitely *don't* let your reader go through your draft silently beforehand. You need the vocal imprint of a genuine first-time reading. A good reader going through a text a *second* time will usually have solved some of the reading problems she encountered initially, and her speaking voice will compensate for them unconsciously, effectively masking them.

3. Take good notes of what you hear in the reading. If that's hard to do at the speed your reader goes, ask her to slow down.

#8

Specifying Feedback

Be wary of the moment you and a helper sit down to talk about your finished draft of a paper. All too often at that point in time, a helper starts calling the shots, in effect telling the writer what aspects of the writing need fixing. Watch for any move a helper makes in that direction. Probably, it will have a friendly sound to it, since most helpers are well-intentioned human beings. It might go like this...

Helper: So what class is this for?

Writer: European History.

Helper (*casually moving the writer's paper from the place on the table in front of the writer, where the writer set it down, to a place in front of himself*): Professor Jasperson?

Writer: O'Rourke.

(*At this point, the helper dives into reading the writer's draft. Two or three minutes go by.*)

Helper: Are you satisfied with your transitions in this paper?

From the hundreds of writer-helper sessions that I've heard over the years, I would be willing to bet good money that this one is doomed. Already, there are signs of a transfer of power from writer to helper. The helper doesn't wait for permission to peruse the writer's paper, he simply takes the paper, physically, away from the writer, to look through it. Just as crucially, the writer makes no effort to articulate his own concerns about the paper—in fact, he speaks a mere three words ("European History," "O'Rourke") in the lead-up to his helper's silent reading. Then, without knowing if transitions are an aspect of the paper that the writer hopes to work on, the helper sets the two of them moving down a path of leading questions *on* transitions

Don't let this happen to you. When you initiate a conversation about your writing—whether by knocking on the door of a friend down the hall or by showing up at a writing center—stay in charge from the word go. Don't take a seat and fall silent, creating a vacuum that the other person will think you want him to fill. Don't issue open-ended invitations like, "I just need someone to check this before I turn it in," or "Would you tell me what you think of this?" In a word, don't present yourself as helpless.

Writers who play helpless learn next to nothing from their interactions with good readers; at best, they leave with somewhat better drafts in hand. An enlightened student's aim isn't "somewhat better drafts," it's real growth in writing skill, which requires being actively involved.

No one gets strong at anything by going somewhere and having it done by someone else. The campus resource most like the writing center is the gym. It would make just about as much sense to go to the gym to find someone to work out *for* you as it would to go to the writing center to have someone revise *for* you. In either case, the long-term gain to you would approach zero. The writing center and the gym exist for people to stretch themselves a bit every time they come. Nobody turns around as a writer on one visit to the writing center, just as no one gets in shape on one visit to the gym. But with many real "workout sessions" at the writing center— or with a classmate or friend who can ably do what a good tutor does—one grows unmistakably more skilled.

If you care about eventually achieving real mastery in writing, here's a plan of action for you: At the beginning of a session with a helper to work on a draft of yours, *you* set the agenda. Depending on what you're concerned about, that agenda might include...

Indicating Level of Engagement

Do you lack confidence that your paper's opening would pique a reader's interest? Have your helper stop reading at the point in your draft where you shift from the opening to the body. Ask her to tell you—on a scale of 1 to 5, where 1 is "not likely at all" and 5 is "very likely"—how likely she would be to read on, if she were not your friend or tutor.

After she does that for you, rather than let her start to make suggestions for revision, tell her what alternatives you've considered. Say, "What if I had opened with my second paragraph?" or "How would it have changed your level of interest if I had taken the incident about gambling on page 3 and hit you with it as my first paragraph, even before broaching the main question of the paper?" or...you get the idea. If she understands the nature of her role, she'll reply, "I'm afraid your second paragraph isn't quite unusual enough to grab me" or, "Oh yeah, that incident—if you left the commentary out— would intrigue me. I'd perk up. I would think, 'What's going on here?'" ...etc.

Forecasting

Organizing prose well is largely a matter of creating expectations and satisfying them—but satisfying them in a way that keeps the reader attentive. If a paper's first paragraph seems to promise an analysis of the reasons for Napoleon's rise to power but the next three paragraphs deal with his wife's taste in clothes, a reader will, at best, feel lost or frustrated and, at worst, feel cheated. At the same time, if a paper's opening telegraphs all the points you plan to make in the paper, a reader is in danger of dozing off by page 3.

In asking someone else to "forecast" your paper, you are asking that person to interrupt her reading of your paper just long enough at the end of each paragraph to say what she believes will happen next. Does she think you're about to state your thesis? To define terms or give background? To launch a presentation of evidence? To refute your opposition? To explain the significance of a long block quote? To do a mid-course summary before shifting to a new, related topic?

Wherever she forecasts incorrectly, you'll want to note that fact and consider whether it calls for re-ordering parts of your paper—or, short of that, for inserting some word or phrase that indicates how your next passage will relate to the one before it, such as "For example..." or "That's just one side of the story, however."

When, on the other hand, she forecasts correctly, you'll occasionally want to mull whether what you've done is too predictable, and therefore dull. Ask her if it is. If she nods, try out some alternatives on her.

Echoing

I don't recall what impelled me to do it, but near the end of the first course in writing I ever taught, I gave my students a list of opinions about writing. Some of these opinions were my own; others were the opposite of mine. I asked my students to underline every statement they could imagine me making.

The results represented the first loud wake-up call of my career. My students would have done better underlining statements at random—despite the fact that they had been assuring me they had perfect understanding of my sermons about writing.

That experience convinced me that to find out if I'm really "getting through" to my audience, I must go further than to ask, "Can you follow me?" Like most yes-or-no questions, it invites laziness. It's easier to nod or to say "yes" than to say "no," which requires explanation. What is more, even when a listener or reader takes it seriously, all I learn from the answer is whether that person can follow what she *believes* my thinking to be; she may be wrong.

So, don't just ask your tutor or friend, "Can you follow my paper?" Ask, instead, "What do you hear me saying in this paper?" See if the response truly echoes your thinking. That's the acid test of clarity.

Handing Down a Verdict

In virtually everything you write, you are advancing a case of some kind, just as a lawyer makes a case in court. This applies not just to papers where you "take a position"—on censorship, gay rights, war in Afghanistan, etc.—but even to autobiographical papers, which need to contain enough vivid details to make events believable. And yet surprisingly few student writers ever ask a reader the big question: "Are you convinced?"

Ask that question. Also, if your helper answers "No," ask these follow-up questions:

> Do I need more evidence?
>
> Is the evidence presented not concrete enough?
>
> Does my logic seem flawed?
>
> Do I fail to acknowledge and sufficiently address an opposing point of view?

Picturing the Writer

Whether a reader gives a piece of writing a fair hearing often depends on the likability or authoritative quality of the writer's voice or "persona." What sort of person do you come across as in your draft? Someone studious? Someone full of spunk? Someone laid-back?

The possibilities are endless, and a good reader can, if you request it, serve as your mirror and tell you what impression you make with your words. Then you and your reader can try to sort out what elements combine to produce that impression—once again, with you in the lead, naming elements that *might be* responsible: diction, connotation, concession (or lack of concession), and so forth.

Cleaning Up

Matters like grammar, punctuation, and spelling should, in my view, wait for last. I care about grammar—I have even written two books on the subject—but not as much as I care about the matters that I've mentioned above: winning reader interest, organizing well (that is, managing the reader's expectations), being clear, being convincing, and letting my voice come through.

When you get around to grammar, don't let your reader become your editor, depriving you of an occasion to increase your own mastery of syntax and punctuation through practice. Either have your reader (a) name the type of error you committed...and give you time to find it by yourself, or (b) mark the location of the error...and give you time to say exactly what the error is and to correct it.

Also, if the errors that your helper finds are numerous, have that person help you make the learning manageable by naming just the two or three types of error that occur most frequently, and by challenging you just to find and correct those. It will be no favor to humanity to let yourself get overwhelmed or to try to fix everything at once. For the sake of your good spirits and success, take it one small batch of issues at a time.

With grammar, as with every other aspect of writing, the more proactively you conduct the sessions that you have with another person, the more you'll learn.

Try This ❯

1. Go to your helper with at least two of the above types of feedback in mind. See what works for you.

2. Alternatively, if you're in a writing class, bring a list of writing criteria (or "rubrics") that your instructor prefers to the list above, and request that your helper give you feedback on two or more issues drawn from that list.

3. Rather than sit idly doing nothing while your helper reads your draft, take the opportunity to give it a fresh reading yourself. It's good exercise in self-critique. (Have a second printout with you.)

4. Time permitting, try to translate your helper's feedback—and your own new discoveries about

your draft, based on re-reading it—into actual revisions of your paper on the spot, while there's still momentum going for you and your helper is still on hand. Do the revisions solve whatever problems you and your helper have flagged? Is the paper more engaging now? More convincing? Etc.

5. If any of your helper's comments don't sit quite right with you (maybe, for example, you don't think that readers other than your helper would be likely to describe the voice of your paper as "irritable"), get yourself a second opinion. All readers, including the best, are idiosyncratic in some ways. Be on guard against feedback that distorts the probable reactions of your readership in general. You, the writer, need to decide which responses to act on and which to let pass.

A Note to Helpers

"Crossing the Line"

No issue comes up more frequently in college writing centers than where to draw the line between helping a writer and taking over from the writer. It can require great self-discipline for a tutor, classmate, or friend to keep that line in view and stay on the correct side of it.

Probably you would agree with me that "taking over" strips the writer of an opportunity to stretch and grow in skill through practice (see my gym analogy on page 59). Even so, when you have a draft before you and spot obvious mistakes in it—a blatant misstatement of fact, a punctuation error, etc.—you may feel an impulse to set things right without delay. As the author H. G. Wells once said, "No passion in the world is equal to the passion to alter someone else's draft."

I am here to tell you, brave it out, resist. Learn to "wait and see" with a writer. Be a supporter on the sidelines of her writing—an engaged, invested voice that propels her down the field but never takes the ball away from her. In due course (not at first but eventually), you'll be surprised by the results she produces.

More specifically:

1. When a writer turns to you for feedback, make it abundantly clear that you'll be happy to oblige. First, though, activate the writer's own revising muscles.

   • As you sit silently reading the writer's draft, have

her do the same with a separate printout of it, for the sake of new discoveries that she may make that way. She has probably not looked at her draft in several hours or a whole day, and stands a better chance now of responding to it as a first-time reader would.

- When both you and she have finished reading her draft, say words to the effect of "Okay, great" (or "I enjoyed your paper"—if you did!), then "Uhh, before I give you *my* feedback, I would love to hear what *you* saw, while re-reading." Nearly always, the writer will emerge from re-reading with a small trove of new observations and thoughts about her draft, thereby both eliminating *your* need to say certain things and, better still, setting you up beautifully to applaud *her* critical acumen.

For example, has the writer asked for feedback on clarity? If so, on re-reading, what sentences or passages does she herself now fear might confuse or mislead a reader? Why?

This maneuver—I call it "gracefully turning the tables on the writer"—is an essential part of nurturing a writer's growth in skill and self-assurance.

2. Only when the writer has exhausted her own diagnostic and problem-solving abilities on the draft at hand—that is, only when the writer has had a good workout—should you give feedback of your own.

3. Even in providing feedback, take care not to assume a directive or superior voice, since such a voice could make the writer deferential to you and, in effect, transfer control of the writing to you. For one thing, don't use evaluative language—the superior tone of a judge—like that you can hear in the margin below:

Judge speaking

Working with infants and toddlers can be a very rewarding experience. One of the most important things you must reflect to the child is the feeling that you are relaxed and comfortable with him. Children are very perceptive, even as infants, and can immediately sense tension and nervousness from an adult.

"*I find your opening weak.*"

"*The indefinite 'you' is not acceptable.*"

"*'Reflect' is incorrect.*"

Also, don't take on the prescriptive tone of a doctor, like that which comes through in the comments in this example:

Doctor speaking

> Working with infants and toddlers can be a very rewarding experience. One of the most important things you must reflect to the child is the feeling that you are relaxed and comfortable with him. Children are very perceptive, even as infants, and can immediately sense tension and nervousness from an adult.

"Cut that first sentence."

"Rather than say 'you,' say 'a child care provider.'"

"Come up with another word here."

Instead, make your comments in a respectful, modest voice that leaves the writer in charge. Speak just as an honest reader, telling the writer what effects her words have had in your head, as below:

Reader speaking

> Working with infants and toddlers can be a very rewarding experience. One of the most important things you must reflect to the child is the feeling that you are relaxed and comfortable with him. Children are very perceptive, even as infants, and can immediately sense tension and nervousness from an adult.

"Who do you mean by 'you'?"

"On first reading, I don't get the meaning of 'reflect.'"

"You've got me hooked here—I want to see how children pick up on adults' feelings toward them. What happened, though, to your first thought, about the work's being rewarding? Was that a throwaway line?"

4. Having delivered feedback like that, revert to the "waiting and seeing" mode. What will the writer now do with what you've said? If, as in the case above, you have reacted to an ambiguous use of the second-person pronoun by asking, "You who?", will the writer herself be able to see the ambiguity in her use of "you"? (That is, will she be able to *diagnose* the writing problem?) Will she then be able to solve the problem, by replacing "you" with a phrase such as "a parent or other caretaker"? Writers will usually rise to the occasion if you play

your cards right. As writing center directors Paula Gillespie and Neal Lerner have written, "Be patient. When you think you've waited long enough, wait that amount of time again.... You'll probably find that the writer was really thinking during those moments and not just staring into space."*

5. To prolong a productive period of silence...

- most of the time, say nothing

- use your body language—for example, lean forward in your seat, and/or keep your eyes focused on the writer's paper—to prevent her from taking your silence as a sign of indifference, and to convey that you are pulling for her

- keep the writer on track by occasionally paraphrasing her own concern, as in

"That word 'reflect' had a meaning in it that you're having trouble finding in another, better word."

or..."Yeah, right, how else could you end this paper?"

- occasionally "check in" with the writer, as in

"How's it coming? Have possible alternatives occurred to you yet? Not yet? That's okay,"

and...

"I'm not going anywhere—take all the time you need."

6. Is there a place for more directive approaches, such as diagnosing a problem ("The reason I get lost here is that I can't tell what 'it' refers to") and posing leading questions ("Can you recall the clever thing you did to eliminate confusion the last time we talked about pronoun reference?")? Yes, there is a place for such moves on your part—in that minority of cases when all the moves above prove insufficient.

My point is, stick to the earlier moves as long as you can. Don't forget that every time you *unnecessarily* diagnose a problem for a writer, you deprive her of an opportunity to practice diagnosis herself, a vital skill in revision—and that every time you *prematurely* point the way to a particular solution to a problem (as, say, with a leading question), you deprive a writer of the chance to practice retrieving and deploying appropriate solutions from the writing repertoire herself, which is a vital reflex to develop.

What You'll Sound Like in Two Months

If you take to heart the advice above, your

development as a writing helper will probably resemble that of Chris Pagnotta, a writing center tutor who, at my request, taped many of his one-to-one meetings with fellow students.

• At the beginning of the semester, you'll do as Chris did in the beginning: you'll just forget my advice. That's how strong the impulse to "fix" mistakes is.

The transcript below, in which Chris refers to a paper with paragraphs that run one and two pages in length, illustrates this first phase of tutoring. Note how Chris, not the writer, flags the problem. Note how Chris invites the writer to comment on the problem Chris has flagged, but then gives the writer less than a second to do so. Note how, in short order, Chris himself revises the paper. Also note who's doing most of the talking (almost all of it, in fact—the writer is reduced to the status of a bystander).

Chris: Okay, I wanted to...ahh.... This paragraph...as a whole?

Writer: Uhuh.

Chris: Ahh, to me, it seems a bit, a bit long.

I don't know how you see it. It, it...there's just a lot of stuff in that paragraph. And the same goes for the second one. I mean, just look. Is there any place in there you think you can maybe cut it? I think it's probably harder for you to see.

Writer: Right.

Chris: But to me there seems to be a place you could maybe do it: [quoting from the writer's paper] "When the management faces a lower or decreasing funding...."

• As the weeks go by and you start noticing that writers have been letting you do all their work for them, you'll decide to make a more concerted effort to translate my advice above into action—but it still won't come easily.

In this next transcript of an exchange between Chris and a writer, listen to how Chris, despite himself, starts again to revise for the writer, then suddenly catches himself and stops, in mid-sentence, in order to shift gears.

Writer: I think I need to work a little more on the conclusion.

Chris: Okay.

Writer: It just didn't sound like a conclusion to me.

Chris: [laughing] I saw that a little bit. I was a little, uhh... [stopping himself from diagnosing the problem and giving his own solution]. What is it that doesn't sound like a conclusion to you?

Writer: In it, I am still explaining things and giving background, instead of wrapping up.

- Finally, with enough self-conscious monitoring like Chris's behind you, a masterful style of "waiting and seeing" (otherwise known as nondirective help) will become second nature to you.

In the session excerpted below, a student arrived wanting Chris just to tell her what to do, but Chris adroitly "turned the tables" on her and employed silence, paraphrase, and checking-in (as in item No. 5 on page 72) to keep the ball in her court. In the end, she solved almost all of her own problems. Here, she comes up for air from a long monologue in which she has reorganized her paper...

Writer: And then I can talk about how I am an

individualist and not a collectivist.... [laughing]
Chris, I am so smart! What would I have done
without you!

Look again at those remarkable two sentences:
"Chris, I am so smart! What would I have done
without you!" They represent the ultimate tribute
to effective "waiting and seeing." Technically, the
second sentence is a non sequitur—a contradiction
of the first. But this writer isn't speaking logically,
she's speaking psycho-logically: what she needed
most was Chris's tacit vote of confidence in her.

* Paula Gillespie and Neal Lerner,
*The Allyn and Bacon Guide to Peer
Tutoring*, 2003, p. 101.

#9

Conducting a Postmortem

Every so often, a student walks into a writing center with a corpse on his hands—a paper that's already been submitted, marked, and graded. Absolutely nothing more can be done for it.

That's a smart move, actually. In all likelihood, the paper in question has been treated roughly by the student's instructor. It has red-inked wounds all over it, and the writer is reeling from the sight of it. How could such a well-intentioned piece of work have come to such a violent end? Wisely, it occurs to the student writer that a good reader may be able to tell him what went wrong, so that he can spare himself more bloodshed in the future.

Initially, the writer in a postmortem sometimes puts the helper on the spot, asking, "Does my paper seem that bad to *you*?" That's a question which the helper may be willing to field, if he is a friend or classmate. If, however, he's a tutor at your writing center, he is likely to deflect it, to avoid being caught in a dispute between student and instructor.

In a postmortem session, the writer will have more success with more specific questions, like:

> What do all these code words in the margin mean—"awk," "comma splice," etc.?
>
> Look, the prof says, "YOU HAVE NO THESIS," but I'd have said I have a thesis at the end of my first paragraph. Doesn't that last sentence qualify as one?
>
> ...Also, she faults me for insufficient evidence. How much evidence is enough?
>
> Why does she say in her note at the end that my paragraphs are too long? Are there rules about how long paragraphs can be?
>
> Isn't "disestablish" a word?

A good helper will have answers to some of these questions, but not all. On those to which he doesn't have answers, he'll probably encourage the writer to speak with his instructor directly. During the entire process, he'll provide the writer with supportive company as they together sort the matter out.

Try This ›

1. As soon as you are done mourning a paper that received a low grade, hand-deliver it to *your* writ-

ing helper—for a proper autopsy.

2. After a postmortem, turn the insights that you glean from it into a checklist for assessing drafts of your *next* paper. Was lack of a clear thesis an issue in Paper No. 1? Take a draft of Paper No. 2 to your helper, and name thesis formulation as one of your concerns from the outset.

3. In addition, set a time for a postmortem on Paper No. 2, so that your helper and you can celebrate how much better it's received than Paper No. 1 was—or, if it is not received better, so that you and your helper can strategize again, in the reasonable hope of celebrating *soon*.

#10

Having a Personal Trainer for a Grammar Self-Assessment

A reason why some college teachers don't use class time to deal with grammar is that no two of their students have precisely the same grammar "profile." One (maybe you) still writes run-on sentences but never misplaces an apostrophe. Another makes apostrophe mistakes and, besides that, often pairs a plural noun with a singular verb.... You get the idea: at the college level, the list of rules *you* have yet to nail isn't likely to be that of any of your classmates.

And yet grammar still matters. Errors in grammar often lead to miscommunication, and, even when they don't, they get noticed by teachers, employers, customers, and the reading public generally, who take a writer down a peg or two in their respect because of such mistakes.

One approach to finding out what grammar rules you personally still need to master is to do a grammar self-assessment with someone strong in grammar. Take these steps:

1. In a book or online, find a good diagnostic test on grammar—if possible, a test that comes with an answer sheet. (Feel free to use the test I have developed, which appears below this list of steps.)

2. Try your hand at the test you choose. Then check your work against the answer sheet, or, if no answer sheet exists, ask your writing helper to correct your responses.

3. Ponder all the places where your own responses don't match the correct ones. **What questions about particular grammar rules do these mismatches raise for you?**

4. Most importantly, follow up step 3 with a leisurely, unembarrassed conversation with your helper. Don't be shy—or afraid to take up too much of your helper's time. Be exhaustive. *Get your questions answered, since doing that is the self-assessment's main purpose.*

   - At times, your helper will instantly be able to answer your question. At other times, she'll know what's right or wrong grammatically but not exactly how to state the reason, since following the rule comes automatically to her now. She may have to grab a handbook off the shelf or go online for a clear explanation of a rule. That's to be expected.

   - Also, please note: not all discrepancies between your own responses and those on an answer sheet indicate an error on your part. Some discrepancies fall into grammar's *gray* area, where different choices, being equally correct, just reflect writers' different styles. (For example, I use parentheses more freely than many writers would, but my parentheses are grammatically correct.)

5. Once you've had your questions answered—but not until then—try your hand at a second diagnostic test covering the same rules (or, in the case of my test, just move on to the second half).

6. Repeat steps 3 and 4 above with that other diagnostic test (or the second half of my test).

7. *Make a checklist of the rules you are still liable to forget about, and consult it in the last, proofreading stage of writing your papers.* Typically, students do better in the second round of a grammar self-assessment than in the first—having had the benefit of a good, clarifying conversation between rounds—but even then, some gaps in mastery typically remain. A checklist will remind you of the rules you personally still tend to forget. If you check it faithfully before submitting final copy of a piece of writing, pretty soon you will have nailed those rules, too.

A Note to Helpers

During step 5 (when the writer is working on the second half of a self-assessment), browse in handbooks or online to find better explanations and examples than the ones that first came to your mind in fielding questions from the writer. Take what you find that way, and work it into the second Q and A session you and the writer have together.

Good online resources include the Purdue OWL (online writing laboratory): owl.english.purdue.edu/

A Grammar Self-Assessment to Try

(It's a short one, covering mistakes made *frequently* at the college level.)

Instructions

A. On pages 88-92, you will see the first half of a long, fictitious letter. Read it, checking for grammar and punctuation.

B. When you find an error, circle it, and use the blank page to the right to say what the error is. (Don't worry about using technical terms.)

C. When you reach the end of Paragraph 6, have a relaxed conversation with your helper about the discrepancies between your marks and those to be found on the "answer sheet" at www.writingdoesnthavetobelonely.com. Only then should you proceed to mark the second half of the letter—also to be found at www.writingdoesnthavetobelonely.com, together with the few remaining steps to follow at that point.

FYI, the second half contains exactly the same types of error the first half contains, so that you can gauge your own improvement between halves.

Dear First-Year Student,

¶1 It seems like only yesterday when I was sitting in your places, wanting to make the best possible use of the time, which remained of my college years. I made some good decisions and others were problematic.

¶2 Now that I am a full-fledged, working accountant, Dean Parker, whom I owe some favors, has called me, and asked me to take a few minutes to reflect on the skills that I *wish* I had developed in my college years'. (She flattered me by saying that she knew that any response of mine would, in her words, "be honest and substantive.)

¶3 When I first heard Dean Parkers request I had no idea what I might write to you about, but then it came to me (naturally enough), when I sat down to do the writing: *writing* was the skill I ought to have learned better in school!

¶4 I am not surprised by my former classmates, when they tell me how much writing they have to do on the job, they however are people who went into fields like history, law, and advertising. I did not go into such a field—or so I thought. In fact, I chose accounting partly to *escape* words.

¶5   Little did I know that even an accountant spends a large fraction of his or her work time writing! Everything from memos and accounting footnotes to shareholder's reports. Needless to say an accountant who can crunch numbers, but cannot state clearly what it means will not do well, clients want something more than the numbers; lucid analysis. They want to know numbers' meaning. For example the profitability of each division of their businesses. Or the tax implications of taking certain losses in one year, instead of to wait. What is more to the point, they want to be told these things clearly and concisely, not to be handed vague language or language so rife with grammatical errors as to distract them or undermine their confidence in the analysis generally. (You might be shocked to see what big effects even small mechanical errors have on a readers assessment of a writer and a writers' competence. Believe it or not off the record I was once informed by a friend that I had been denied a certain job interview on the basis of my letter of application for it in which I had carelessly mixed up "there" and "their".)

¶6   I have been lucky at the firm of Miller and Khalil. The reason being that my supervisor there edits my drafts of memos, gives me writing handbooks to review, and even tutors me at times. As a result, it now seems to

him and I that I've made progress—or what he kindly calls "progress and a half". However, I cannot stress this enough: with almost any other supervisor, I would now be worrying about keeping my job. When it comes to writing a prospective employee should not expect "on-the-job training"; once again, I have been lucky.

Reminder: the answer sheet for this half of the letter—together with the unmarked second half of this letter and further instructions—can be found at www.writingdoesnthavetobelonely.com.

outage

...wages, and food that had to
...ded, but the company

...il, crews have been work...
...d a second transformer
...d substation, NSt...
...hael Durand said.
...omplex process,
...it was not clea...
...unit failed, tri...

BACK BAY, P...

Woman gets jail for teens drinking

Beverly mother hosted party; served minors

DA calls tough sentence a prom season warnin...

By Mark Arsenaul...
GLOBE STAFF

Alli Knothe, and Am...
GLOBE CORRESPON...

BEVERLY — In t...
...tempted to Sale...

#11

Having a Personal Trainer — for Stimulus Exchanges

Improvement as a writer, just like improvement as an acrobat or surgeon, takes practice. If you're someone who sincerely wants to leave college with high-order skills of expression, let a writing helper provide you with a verbal workout beyond what you can get from classes alone. Regularly meet with a classmate, friend, or tutor, and, each time that you meet, select a writing stimulus—an image or short text that strikes you as provocative. Then, make that stimulus your subject in a mini-essay of 100-200 words.

If your helper is a person who, like you, wants to keep getting better at writing, he or she will be more than happy to write separately on the same stimulus while you're writing, since a stimulus exchange benefits writers at all levels of proficiency.

Possible types of stimuli include the ones laid out below, on pages 96-99.

an intriguing (or upsetting) photograph or work of art

For example:

Photo: Hart Day Leavitt

Good sources of photography and art include:

- numerous books in your school library

- a Google site of more than one billion photos, accessible by Googling the phrase "documentary photos images" (To single out an image and enlarge it, click on it and use your computer's zoom feature.)

- the online site bridgemanart.com. (Bridgeman sells the rights to art images, but doesn't charge just for looking. Don't sign in. Go straight to the search bar and type in a topic that interests you—such as "conflict" or "holidays." A slew of small images will fill the screen. To single out an image and enlarge it, click on it.)

a news article

For example:

Balloon Flight Was Hoax, Court Is Told
The mother of the 6-year-old boy once thought to have been carried away by a runaway helium balloon has admitted that the episode was a hoax. According to court documents released yesterday,....

—Dan Elliott, Associated Press

Good sources of the latest news include:

- magazines and newspapers in your school library

- the online editions of newspapers that haven't yet gone to a paid subscription basis online. (That's too changeable a list to put in print here.)

a provocative quotation

For example:

Here lies Maggie Kuhn under the only stone she left unturned.

—Epitaph of Well-Known Elder Activist

> Good sources of quotations include countless online sites. To access them, Google "quotations."

an opening line for a short story (if fiction is among the types of writing that interest you to work on)

For example:

As he sat reading, Antoine stumbled on a small, handwritten comment in the margin of his used copy of the book assigned in History 110. The comment seemed unrelated to history.

> For other openers:
> - browse in a book of short stories
> - ask your helper to come up with some.

two or three unrelated rhyme words to use in the same short poem (if you're a would-be poet).

For example:

canned/understand*

mow/portfolio

necklace/feel less

> For other unusual rhyme pairs, go to http://rhymebrain.com/en and type in any word that occurs to you. A list of words that rhyme with your word will appear instantly.
>
> For a good, long list of ways to prompt poetry that don't involve rhyming, go to http://www.david.com/thejournal/tjresources-exercises.php#poetry.

Try This ›

1. When you find a helper to do stimulus exchanges with you, choose a first stimulus from the sources above. Then, don't just dive in and write: name the aspects of your writing you personally hope to improve in the process, and suggest that your helper do the same. Your many options include:

___ fluency in English   ___ clarity/precision

___ argumentation   ___ sentence variety

___ voice   ___ metaphor

___ vividness   ___ conciseness

___ suspense   ___ humor

You can probably name others:

The importance of taking this preliminary step of naming a goal can't be overstated. The driver of a car is unlikely to reach her destination if she hasn't named that place in her mind and remained conscious of it while driving. The advantage here is what people call "the power of intention."

2. Whatever aims you name, self-consciously work *toward* them as you write.

For example, look again at the scene of a cat and mouse above.

• If your aim is to construct better arguments, you might use the scene as evidence to support the thesis "Often, it is hard to tell playfulness from malice."

• If your aim is to be vivid or suspenseful, you might try to capture the sheen of the cat's black hair...and how the cat contents itself (for now, at least) with extending a long paw just to touch the mouse's short tail...and how the blur produced by the cat's *own* tail, as it slaps the floor, conveys an excitement that could "turn ugly" anytime.

3. Once you and your helper have written on-the-spot responses to a stimulus, share them with each other:

   • Read them silently or out loud.

   • Remind one another of your writing aims.

   • Give each other honest feedback—especially about how close the writing comes to achieving your aims.

---

*One poem that a student wrote from this prompt was entitled "The Sardine."

I don't have to be canned
To understand.
I don't have to be eaten—
I've took a beatin'.
So, have a haddock,
'Cause I've had it.

12

Having a Personal Trainer — for Games

Benjamin Franklin (who is featured in Chapter 13) believed playing chess developed a person's ability to think ahead and to persevere. Similarly, other people have attributed the acquisition of important life skills to games ranging from Twenty Questions to poker.

We don't necessarily play games in order to develop ourselves, but our self-development is often a side benefit. Something about the rules-based, friendly competition of a game draws us in and mildly addicts us, and, without our thinking much about it, we eventually get better at the skill the game requires.

Below I describe two games you can play with a helper to develop *writing* skills.

Word Salad (for mastering a wider range of ways to construct a sentence)

Rounds 1-4*

The object is simple to state: Be the player who can use the largest number of listed words in a single, perfectly grammatical sentence. (There is at least one perfectly grammatical sentence that uses all the words in a list—but even a strong writer would have trouble getting it.)

Feel free to insert any punctuation needed, as well as to capitalize the first letter of a word. However, don't change the tense of verbs or switch between singular and plural nouns or pronouns.

Round 1	Round 2	Round 3	Round 4
and	abilities	a	a
and	and	a	a
and	athletes	allergic	and
are	beginning	Anastasia	and
become	dedication	any	at
books	fans	before	be
books	field	but	between
bookstores	had	cold	can
brick	hard	feeling	college
convenient	have	for	colleges
costly	in	had	difference
digital	is	had	except
electronic	just	having	few
I	native	house	graduate
in	of	in	instruction

increasing	of	Jim's	level
less	of	minutes	little
light	on	never	no
media	own	of	people
more	result	other	offer
mortar	see	reaction	or
of	since	repeatedly	relatively
of	sports	she	smaller
of	steroids	she	tell
often	the	sneezed	tend
other	the	something	that
physical	the	such	the
popularity	the	suspected	the
than	they	symptoms	to
the	to	there	to
what	truly	three	university
which	use	to	you
will	what	was	
wonder	whether	without	
	wonder		
	work		

(34 words)	(36 words)	(34 words)	(32 words)

*For additional rounds, go to
 www.writingdoesnthavetobelonely.com.

At about twenty minutes into a round, have your rival player, the helper, finish her work on the round and do the following for you:

1. look up the mystery sentence—the sentence that contains every word in the round—which can be found at www.writingdoesnthavetobelonely.com.

2. tell you (at a time you name for a break) one or two of the grammatical features of the mystery sentence, using non-technical language like that below:

> The mystery sentence opens with a long string of words starting with "since."
>
> In the middle of the sentence is a *series* of items.
>
> The "-ing" word in the sentence may look like a verb, but it's a noun.
>
> The sentence is a question, not a statement.
>
> The sentence's flow is interrupted by a definition, a phrase that comes right after an uncommon word in the sentence to explain what that word means.

Do such clues help? Usually they do. More importantly, they increase a player's consciousness of options available to him whenever he writes.

Finally, when you feel you've used as many of the words in a round as you can, show your sentence to your helper and have your helper show hers to you.

Who won? That is, who wrote the longer, perfectly grammatical sentence? (Of course, the helper in this game plays at something of a disadvantage, since she has to stop work on the round before clues are available.)

Are there sentence elements you used that you're proud of, since they haven't come automatically to you in the past? Saying them aloud will help you to consolidate your knowledge of those elements. They'll be that much more accessible to you the next time you need them in your writing.

What stumbling blocks did you encounter? For example, did it seem to you that there were too few verbs at your disposal in the round? Too many *a's* and *the's* to find places for? When you see the mystery sentence, can you tell what grammatical moves the original author made that you, too, could have made, to eliminate those stumbling blocks?

Half-Baked (for developing more effective word choice and other writing strengths)

The object of Half-Baked is to fool your opponent into believing that something partly written by you was written entirely by a published author.

Instructions

1. Go through an anthology of good prose readings until you find a reading whose opening paragraph or two you like. Ideally, the passage would come in under 100 or 150 words in length.

2. Type that passage on a computer.

3. Copy and paste that passage to a second page.

4. On the second page, feel free to cut as much of the original text as you believe you might be able to replace with equally good (or better) language of your own. Also, feel free to reorganize the passage.

   Don't bother counting the number of words you cut, but do keep a tally of the number of words you come up with to *replace* the words you cut. (The reason for doing this will become clear shortly.)

5. Show your opponent both versions—the original version and your own, doctored version—but without saying which is which. Let your opponent *guess* which is which.

6. A player wins if her opponent mistakes her doctored version for the true original.

However, in a great many rounds, either both players guess right or both guess wrong—there's a tie. *In those cases, the winner of the round is the player whose doctored version of the original contains the highest number of her own, inserted words.*

The strategic challenge of the game can be stated this way: Generally speaking, the more that a player uses words of her own in her doctored version, the easier time her opponent will have to spot her version for the phony that it is. On the other hand, the *less* that she uses words of her own, the less opportunity she'll have to win in the frequent case of a tie.

7. Most importantly in terms of learning, save a few minutes at the end of each round to pinpoint where a player's new version went right or wrong.

Could you spot the true original?

Below are two passages that a student handed me when he and I were playing Half-Baked. Would you be able to say which was the original, published version?

> Airplanes are such a common form of travel that it's easy to forget just how recently they were invented. Today, even a person in the middle of nowhere would not be surprised to see a plane in the sky. But before the Wright Brothers flew their plane at Kitty Hawk, North Carolina, in 1903, most scientists thought flight by heavier-than-air machines would never be achieved. Never. In fact, the word airplane didn't come into common usage until after 1945.
>
> ....
>
> Airplanes are such a common form of travel that it's easy to forget just how recently they were invented. Before the Wright Brothers flew their plane at Kitty Hawk, North Carolina, in 1903, flight by heavier-than-air machines was thought impossible. In fact, the word airplane didn't come into common usage until after 1945. Now in 2009, there are over 15,000 airports in the U.S. alone, meaning that even the most rural dweller would not be surprised to see a plane in the sky.

Did you pick the second version as the original? That's what I did, but the first is the true original.

What threw me off? The student author of the second version had astutely moved events into chronological order ("before 1903"--+1903--+"after 1945"--+2009), making them much easier for me to follow. He had also shrewdly inserted the number of airports in the U.S., lending persuasive force to the claim that everyone alive sees planes in the sky.

But to be honest, I've been tricked many times by students playing Half-Baked with me, and each time seems to yield a new writing insight.

#13

Having a Personal Trainer — for Ben Franklin's Exercise

If you're someone wanting to achieve a stylistic break-
through in your writing, you could do worse than to adopt
the regimen that that old self-improver Ben Franklin once
devised for himself and described in his autobiography.

My free adaptation:

Day 1

1. Talk with your writing helper about the ways you'd like
   to improve as a writer, and see if, between you, you
   can come up with a short list of authors who exem-
   plify those writing qualities—maybe George Orwell for
   description in his colonial memoirs, maybe Ariana Huff-
   ington for social commentary with "attitude" or humor.

2. In a print anthology or online, find a good short piece
   by that author. Copy it or print it out.

3. Select a good excerpt from within the piece, aiming for
   a text of 150-200 words.

4. Turn your chosen passage into a set of notes. Using your own words, record each fact or idea found in the passage on a separate note card or sheet of paper.

Suppose, for instance, that the first three sentences of your passage read as follows:

> All sitcoms on TV once dished out the same tepid fare. An easily avoidable misunderstanding or small crisis would rapidly develop in the characters' home or workplace. It would then neatly resolve itself just in time for a laugh-track-riddled half hour to give way to cloying theme music and the final credits.

Your notes on these sentences might look like this:

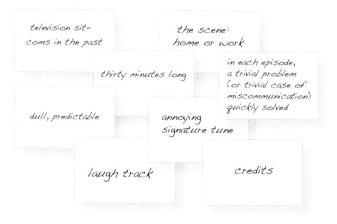

- television sit-coms in the past
- the scene: home or work
- thirty minutes long
- in each episode, a trivial problem (or trivial case of miscommunication) quickly solved
- dull, predictable
- annoying signature tune
- laugh track
- credits

5. Shuffle your notes and put them away, or give them to your helper for safekeeping.

Day 2 (not necessarily the next day)

1. Look through your notes. Put them in the best order you can come up with.

2. Write as strong a passage as you can, based on your notes.

3. After you finish, pull out the published original version again and compare it with your own version. *Do this in conversation with your writing helper.*

   In what respects is the published original a more effective piece of writing? In what respects is *your* passage more effective?

   What details of sequence or style seem to account for these differences?

Woman gets jail for teens drinking

Beverly mother hosted party, served minors

DA calls tough sentence a prom season warning

By Mark Arsenault

GUEST STAFF

Alli Knothe, and Ama

GLOBE CORRESPONDENT

BEVERLY — In

attempted to

Wozzle

#14

Combining Types of Help

You can avail yourself of ideas in this book one-at-a-time or in combinations. When it comes to combination, the possibilities are endless:

- You could make a **writing "date"** and *follow* it with getting **mentored.**

- You could use a classmate, friend, or tutor to help you **pace yourself** and, depending on what stage in the writing process you were checking in about on a certain day, you could also use that person as a **sounding board,** or as your respondent in a **silent dialogue.**

- You could arrange to meet with a tutor on Tuesdays for a **stimulus exchange** and on Fridays for a **game.**

Writing doesn't have to be a lonely activity.

Letter to Instructors

We teachers of writing die at least twice yearly. In December and again in May, we vanish from our latest students' sight forever, with the task unfinished. We and they alike privately wonder, "Who, if anyone, is out there to pick up where the teaching left off?"

What, to my mind, justifies having our students read a book like this is that it answers that question.

I certainly don't wish to ignore other, shorter-term reasons one may have for assigning such a book. Maybe, for example, your students do peer editing in class—or consult with peers about their writing at a campus writing center—and you'd like to give them guidance about getting the most possible out of these occasions. As a teacher and the former director of two college writing centers, I applaud your interest. I would like to think this book serves the worthy aim you have in mind.

That said, however, the main thing motivating me to pen *Writing Doesn't Have to Be Lonely* was the reality that at each semester's end we disappear for good from our students' lives. In all probability, the first-year "comp" class that you teach will be the last opportunity your students have for formal instruction in writing, despite the fact that they have only just begun to realize their potential as writers. **If, in future years, they are to sustain and build upon the progress that they make with you, they are going to need a repertoire of ways to use other people for support, advice, and feedback in their writing. This book's purpose is to provide students with that lifelong repertoire.**

If you have been browsing in the book, you already know that it contains fourteen short chapters, each devoted to a different way to include other people in one's writing process. If you haven't yet browsed in it, a thirty-second look at the table of contents—with its titles that range from "Writing Date" to "Grammar Self-Assessment"—will give you some idea of the variety of modes of writer-helper interface promoted in these pages.

As an instructor, you could, for instance, **have students find a classmate, friend, or writing center tutor who would try out a specific number of these modes with them during the semester—**

- maybe all fourteen

- maybe six or seven of your choice, or of your students' choice

- maybe two modes drawn from pages 11-51 (related to the pre-drafting and drafting phases of writing), two drawn from pages 53-81 (related to the revision phase), and two drawn from pages 83-115 (on writing skills in general).

Also, you could **have students append postscripts to their papers,** in which they...

- describe what they have tried

- honestly assess its payoff to them in terms of both how well their papers came out and (not to be neglected) how much they enjoyed the writing process

- and say what they might do differently the next time they adopt the same mode.

Over a career spanning four decades, one thing hasn't changed: the most common first utterance of a first-time user of a college writing center. It goes, "Could you look this paper over for grammar?" Few first-timers have a clear conception of the diverse ways writers use their fellow writers and good readers. They appear at a writing center only after they've produced a draft—thereby sadly by-passing all the very fruitful forms of help available to them before drafting—and they initially confine their requests for help in the revision phase to grammar and citation form. By and large, outside of the students who become writing center regulars, the graduates of our schools have not been made aware of most of the most powerful uses of a second person in the writing process. If we care about their future growth as writers, we ought to give them good, class-related practice in the whole array of types of "friendly exploitation of others." With such practice, they would have the means to extend their growth as writers over whole lifetimes.

Lawrence Weinstein

Acknowledgments

It should hardly be surprising that a man who advocates getting help with writing has many good people to thank at the end of his book. I just hope I don't forget too many.

The Bentley University peer tutors who have given me invaluable feedback on each draft of it—and/or let me photograph them with fellow students at our writing center—include Chris Brault, Kristy Callahan, Stephanie Davenport, Angela Diaco, Emily DiGiovanna, Rick DiLorenzo, Josh Foster, Kaylyn Frazier, Ryan Gilette, Jen Johnson, Steve Jones, Vijay Maharaj, Will Markow, Rob Mills, Cassandra Morello, Will Pang, Yulia Podolny, Alec Russell, Andy Roque, Katie Spinello, Jonathan Tetrault, Tammie Vicente, and Mark Zurlo.

Without input from these students and Prof. Gregory Farber-Mazor, my worthy successor at the Bentley Writing Center, this compendium would be both far less clear than it is and less in line with "facts on the ground."

My chief editor (not to mention everlasting mainstay) has been my wife, Diane Albert Weinstein, and my "Devil's Advocate" (see pages 43-45 above) has been my not-uncritical but very loyal brother, Warren Weinstein.

I am indebted, as well, to the gifted designer of this book, Tom Briggs, with whom collaboration has been a true pleasure.

L.W.

Author Bio

Lawrence Weinstein taught the first-year writing course at Harvard University from 1973 to 1983 and cofounded Harvard's Writing Center. Since then, he has been a member of the English Department at Bentley University, where he has served long stints directing both the Writing Center and the Expository Writing Program. His book on the teaching of writing, *Writing at the Threshold*, is a longtime bestseller of the National Council of Teachers of English (NCTE).

Other books by Weinstein include *Grammar for the Soul* (Quest Books, 2008) and *Grammar Moves*, a textbook version of *Grammar for the Soul* written with his colleague Thomas Finn (Pearson, 2010). Soon to be released is his anthology of readings for college-level writing classes, *Money Changes Everything* (Bedford, St. Martins, 2013).

Weinstein's plays have been performed in Boston, Dallas, and New York. His own favorite is *The LaVidas' Landlord*.

He welcomes mail sent to lweinstein@bentley.edu.